Eat with Intention:

A 30-Day Guide to Mindful Eating and Joyful Living"

By Michelle Will.

Table of contents

Introduction: The Power of Mindful Eating

Welcome to your journey of discovery - a path that leads to a healthier, happier you through the simple act of eating with intention. Have you ever wolfed down a meal without really tasting it? Or found yourself munching mindlessly while watching TV? Don't worry, we've all been there. But what if I told you there's a better way to nourish your body and soul?

Let's talk about mindful eating. It's not just a fancy term - it's a life-changing approach to food that can transform your health from the inside out. Imagine this: you're sitting down to a meal, and instead of rushing through it, you take the time to really experience your food. You notice the colors on your plate, breathe in the delicious smells, and savor each bite like it's a little treasure. That's mindful eating in action!

Now, you might be wondering, "That sounds nice, but what's in it for me?" Well, buckle up, because the benefits of mindful eating are pretty amazing:

1. Your tummy will thank you: When you eat slowly and pay attention, your digestive system doesn't have to work overtime. This means less tummy trouble and more energy for fun!

2. Goodbye, extra pounds: By listening to your body's signals, you're less likely to overeat. Many people find they reach a healthy weight without strict diets.

3. Happy mind, happy life: Mindful eating can help chase away worries about food. It's like giving your brain a mini-vacation at every meal!

4. Smarter food choices: When you really tune in, you'll naturally want foods that make your body feel good. Your taste buds might even start craving fruits and veggies!

5. Steady energy all day: Mindful eating helps keep your blood sugar on an even keel. No more afternoon slumps!

6. More yum, less glum: When you truly enjoy your food, you often need less to feel satisfied. It's like getting more bang for your bite!

7. Better relationship with food: Say farewell to feeling bad about what you eat. Mindful eating helps you make peace with food.

Now, I know what you're thinking - "This sounds great, but how do I do it?" Don't fret! That's exactly why we're here. Over the next month, we'll explore fun and easy ways to bring mindful eating into your life. We'll learn how to listen to our bodies, deal with tricky emotions around food, and create habits that stick.

Remember, this isn't about being perfect. It's about making small changes that add up to big results. Some days will be easier than others, and that's okay. Think of it like learning to ride a bike - you might wobble at first, but soon you'll be cruising!

So, are you ready to start this exciting adventure? Let's turn the page and begin our journey to mindful eating and joyful living. Your body and mind are in for a treat - literally! Get ready to transform your relationship with food, one mindful munch at a time. Trust me, in the future you will be doing a happy dance!

Chapter 1: Understanding Mindful Eating

Hey there, food explorer! All set to go into the realm of mindful eating? Now let's dissect it together.

What is mindful eating?

Consider yourself dining at a luxury restaurant. The server brings out a lovely dinner platter. You take in the scent, pause to appreciate it, then gently bite first. You notice how the tastes dance on your tongue. In essence, that's mindful eating!

The essence of mindful eating is being present with your meal. It's not about imposing rigid guidelines or self-restraint. Rather, it's about: paying attention to your food with all your senses; eating deliberately and enjoying each mouthful; listening to your body's hunger and fullness signals;

selecting meals that make you feel good; eating without distractions (bye-bye, TV dinners!)

The advantages of mindful eating

You might be asking right now, "Why bother?" Mindful eating, therefore, has several wonderful advantages:

1. Eating slowly and chewing carefully helps your gut to absorb food more easily.

2. Weight control: You're less prone to overindulge by listening to your body's instincts.

3. Better connection with food: There's no more guilt trips about your diet!

4. When you actually pay attention, food tastes so much better.

5. Less stress: Mindful eating may be a kind of meditation that helps you to relax.

6. Improved nutrition: You usually choose better when you know what you're eating.

Typical misinterpretations

Let's clean some murky rivers before we go any more:

 Myth 1: Mindful eating is a diet.
Truth: It's about altering your eating, not about limiting food.

Myth 2: You have to eat very slowly constantly.
Truth: Though slow eating is beneficial, mindful eating is more about awareness than pace.

Myth 3: You will never be able to eat in front of the TV once again.

Truth: The objective is not to never multitask but rather to become more conscious. Start modest then expand from there.

Myth 4: Mindful eating lets you eat anything you want.
Truth: Though it's not about limitation, mindful eating nevertheless requires awareness of how certain meals impact your body.

Myth 5: It takes much too long.
Truth: Even if lunch only lasts 15 minutes, you can practice mindful eating. It's about quality, not count.

Thus, you now have your introduction to mindful eating. It's about being present; it's not about perfection. The following chapters will explore further ways to include this practice into your everyday life. All set to savor the next mouthful of this fantastic trip? Let's head off!

chapter 2: Getting Ready For Your 30-Day Journey

Hi explorer! Welcome You are about to start a wonderful journey into the field of mindful eating. We have to prepare and pack our baggage, just like any major journey does. So let's get ready for this wonderful 30-day adventure by rolling up our sleeves!

Creating Your Plans

Let us first discuss your reasons for being here. Get a notepad and write your responses to these questions:

1. How did you come across this book?
2. By the conclusion of these thirty days, what do you want your attitude to food to be?
3. In your eating patterns, what one little adjustment would you like?

These are your goals; your own North Star to help you over this path. Keep them near, much like a beloved map. These goals will remind you why you began when the road becomes a little rocky (and it may).

Creating Your Oasis for Mindful Eating

Let us now arrange your surroundings to enable your next journey. Imagine it as creating a comfortable treehouse for your gut and psyche!

1. Look at your dining areas to clear clutter:Are sheets covering your kitchen table? Is your workstation also an eating space? Time for a little cleaning session! Clear areas enable clear thinking.

2. Stock Goodness: Load your refrigerator and pantry with things your body will feel fantastic. You want to be ready, just like you

would want to carry the proper tools for a trek!

3. Look for a unique bowl or dish that makes you grin to set the mood. Perhaps keep a candle burning during meals. These tiny details may make dining a memorable occasion.

4. Set aside mealtimes as a "no phone zone" and unplug to tune in. Though at first strange, give it a try. Your gut and your food will appreciate you for the whole undivided attention.

Getting Your Toolkit for Mindful Eating

Every hero, therefore, needs his tools. Your mindful eating tool here is:

1. One reliable friend is a journal. Jot down your ideas, emotions, and food-related revelations here.

2. A Timer: To help you to calm down rather than to hurry you! Try scheduling it for twenty minutes per meal.

3. Your Senses: These have always been your always! On this road, we will be heavily employing them.

4. Comfy Clothes: Your buddy here is elastic waistbands. We want you to be at ease and capable of noticing messages from your body.

5. Patience and kindness are your abilities. Recall—you are picking up a new ability. Take care of yourself gently.

Getting Ready for Takeoff

Let's conduct a last check before we soar out on our 30-day journey:

1. Set aside some time on your calendar just for eating. Eating on demand is quite last season!
2. Share with your housemates or family your path. They might wish to participate!
3. Snap a "before" view of your plate. Compared to your "after" in thirty days, it will be interesting.
4. Most crucially, bring your curiosity. We will look at the wonderful world you and your relationship with food inhabit.

Are you prepared? Recall, this trip is not about perfection. It's about development, learning, and maybe some laughter along the road. You are right! We will first enter the amazing realm of mindful eating tomorrow. You rest, courageous adventurer; your journey is only waiting!

Chapters 3: The Mind-Body Connection

Hey mind-body explorer! Want to pick up the secret language your body and brain use to talk about food? Get ready since we will start an incredible trip inside each of us!

Feast of Emotion

Your feelings can be like cunning chefs developing appetites and changing the taste of food. As it is! Let us tour this emotive kitchen:

1. **Happy Chef**: On cloud nine food could taste extra delicious. Ever noticed how amazing celebration food tastes?

2. **Stress Chef**: This disorganized cook could make you crave sugary or salted delicacies. Your body seems to be cuddling itself with food.

3. **Sad Chef**: When you're blue you could lose appetite or resort to comfort foods. Your body is lifting you.

4. **Bored Chef**: This sly chef could make you want to bite even if you're not really hungry. It merely seeks some thrills.

Period of Activities:

Keep a "Mood Food Diary" for a few days. Sort your emotions before you eat. You might uncover some quite interesting patterns!

The Growing-Tummy Telegraph

Your body gives signals regarding diet all the time. Still, sometimes it seems as though it is speaking another dialect! Let's work through these signals:

Growing tummy; feeling a bit weak or agitated; thinking about food a lot; hunger signals

Food tastes less interesting today; you feel energized instead of sleepy; you are not stuffed and instead rather happy.

Think of those signals as whispers. We have to calm ourselves and really pay attention to hear them!

Try:
On a 1–10 rating system, rate your hunger before your next meal. Proceed similarly after eating. This helps you become aware of messages from your body.

Your Plate and The Stress Monster

Stress can be like a cheeky monster upsetting your eating pattern. The following is how:

1. It could entirely eliminate your appetite or cause great hunger.

2. It can cause you to want bad foods—hello, ice cream for dinner!

3. It could cause you to eat without fully experiencing your cuisine and too quickly.

Still, rest not! We are armed with some stress-busting strategies:

Before eating, inhale deeply. It's like giving your stress monster a time-off. Eat without looking around. Turn off the TV and slide your phone away. Chew carefully and truly taste your food. It reminds me of a little meditation.

Combining All Things

Your body and mind are best buddies that constantly discuss food. Through listening to this dialogues, you can:

1. Know why you choose the foods you do.

2. Learn to eat when you are really hungry.

3. stop when you are comfortably full.

4. Select foods that satisfy your intellect as well as your body.

Recall, this mind-body connection is personal to you. It's okay if what your friend finds working doesn't apply to you! This road is mostly about learning YOUR body and mind better.

As we close this chapter, stop and consider your incredible physique. All of this time, we have been speaking with you! Learning to listen now will help you to develop fluency in the language of mindful eating.

We will next pick some interesting approaches to apply this mind-body wisdom. Prepare to be a mindful eating super hero!

Chapter 4: Mindfulness Techniques for Eating

Welcome to your toolbox of mindful eating tricks! Today, we're going to explore some nifty techniques that'll transform your meals from ordinary to extraordinary. Think of these as your secret weapons for becoming a mindful eating superhero!

Breathe Before You Bite

First up, let's talk about the power of your breath. It's like a magic wand that can calm your mind and prepare your body for a meal. Here's a fun exercise to try:

The Five-Breath Reset:
1. Sit comfortably in front of your meal.
2. Close your eyes (no peeking at your yummy food yet!).
3. Take a deep breath in through your nose, counting to five.

4. Hold it for a moment, then slowly breathe out through your mouth, counting to five again.
5. Repeat this five times.

Tada! You've just hit the reset button on your brain. You're now ready to eat with a calm mind and a happy tummy.

Sensory Spectacular

Next, let's wake up those senses of yours! Eating isn't just about taste - it's a full-body experience. Try this sensory adventure with your next meal:

1. Look: What colors do you see on your plate? Is your food shiny, dull, or somewhere in between?
2. Smell: Take a big whiff. What scents can you pick out? Does it remind you of anything?
3. Touch: If appropriate, touch your food. Is it smooth, rough, or squishy?

4. Listen: Does your food make any sounds when you move it around?
5. Taste: Finally, take a bite. What flavors dance on your tongue?

By tuning into all your senses, you're turning mealtime into a thrilling exploration. It's like being a food detective!

The Chew Choo Train

Now, let's talk about chewing. It might sound silly, but how you chew can make a big difference in your mindful eating journey. Try this:

The 30-Chew Challenge:
1. Take a bite of food.
2. Start counting your chews.
3. Try to reach 30 chews before swallowing.
4. Notice how the taste and texture change as you chew.

It might feel weird at first, but stick with it. You're giving your taste buds a front-row seat to the flavor show!

Eating Meditation: A Mini Vacation for Your Mind

Lastly, let's try a simple eating meditation. It's like a mini-vacation for your mind, right at your dining table!

1. Take a small bite of food.
2. Close your eyes.
3. Focus all your attention on the food in your mouth.
4. Notice the taste, texture, and how it changes as you chew.
5. Swallow when you're ready, and pause before taking another bite.

Repeat this for a few bites. You might be surprised at how intense the flavors become when you give them your full attention!

Practice Makes Progress

Remember, these techniques might feel a bit strange at first. That's okay! It's like learning to ride a bike - it takes practice. Try one technique at a time, and see which ones you like best. You don't have to use all of them at every meal. Even using one for a few bites can make a big difference.

Your Mindful Eating Challenge:

For the next week, try to use at least one of these techniques at each meal. Keep track of your journal. Which one was your favorite? Did you notice anything new about your food?

Remember, there's no right or wrong way to eat mindfully. The goal is to be more aware and to enjoy your food more. So have fun with it! Who knows? You might discover you're a natural-born food explorer!

Next up, we'll talk about how to handle tricky situations that might pop up on your mindful eating adventure. But for now, go forth and eat with all your senses! Your taste buds are in for a treat!

Chapter 5: Juggling Difficulties

Hey there, mindful muncher! Although right now you have been performing fantastic, let's face it: life isn't always a straight ride. We occasionally run across a few puffs along the road. But don't panic! This chapter will teach us how to negotiate those challenging circumstances that could arise on your path of mindful eating. Consider it your own personal journey map for overcoming culinary obstacles!

Managing Craves: The Sneaky Food Ninjas

Ever felt as though your name was called from a chocolate bar? Alternatively that bag of chips was muttering, "Eat me!" Those are desires, and they may be really clever. Here's how you outsmart them:

1. Imagine your need as a large wave in the ocean. Try to ride it out rather than battle it. Breathe deeply and tell yourself, "This is simply a need. It'll pass." And, guess what? Typically it does!

2. The Distraction Dance: Perform a small, literally-based dance when a craving strikes. Alternatively arrange a quick game or phone a friend. Sometimes all you need is a little diversion to help the need fade.

3. If you choose to consume what you are yearning for, do so deliberately. Especially the taste. You could discover that a little bit satisfies you more than you would have guessed!

Eating in Social Context: The Peer Pressure Mystery

While eating with friends and relatives can be rather enjoyable, it can also complicate mindful eating. These ideas will help you keep on target:

1. The pre-game plan calls for a quick food before you go. This helps you to eat deliberately as you won't be hungry when you get there.

2. Look ahead of time if at all possible the menu detective. This allows you time to consider your actual wants rather than those of others.

3. Aim to be the last person to complete your dinner—the slow-mo eater. Spend some time, talk with friends, and savor the event.

4. Ninja's "No, Thank You" Saying no to meals you dislike or if you're full is reasonable. Start saying, "No, thank you," smiling. With effort, it becomes simpler!

Overcoming Emotional Eating: The Flange Food Fiasco

We eat sometimes not because we're hungry but rather because we're bored, depressed, stressed, or happy. That is known as emotional eating. Here's how you approach it:

When you feel like eating, consider, "Am I really hungry, or am I feeling something else?" Name the feeling you are experiencing, try here.

Create a list of activities you could do when experiencing certain emotions. unfortunate? Perhaps Mom's or Dad's hug would be beneficial. Not bored? Try either painting a picture or reading a book.

Check where you stand before you eat on the Hunger Scale, which runs 1 to 10: 1 is starving, 10 is stuffed. Eat when you're at a three or four; stop at a six or seven.

Talk to yourself as though you would to a dear friend. Rather than "I shouldn't eat this," try "I'm feeling anxious. Right now, what truly do I need?

Recall that it's acceptable if you don't get it perfect every time. Like any ability, mindful eating is one that requires practice. The vital thing is to keep on trying!

Your Mindful Navigator's Challenge:

Try to notice this week when you encounter one of these difficulties. Note in your diary:
1. Describe the circumstances.
2. Your approach was what?
3. What produced success?
4. What might you attempt differently the next time?

By the end of the week, you will have your own method guide for negotiating challenging dining circumstances!

We will then look at how to choose foods that satisfy your body and boost your mood. For now, though, go forth and beat those food obstacles just like the mindful eating champion you are! Recall that every obstacle you encounter is only another opportunity for you to develop on your path of mindful eating. You possess this!

Chapter 6: Feeding Your Body

Welcome, fellow food explorer! Today is a fantastic trip to learn how to feed our bodies with delicious, wholesome meals. Consider your body as a super-cool machine; it needs the proper type of fuel to work without problems. Let's get right into learning how to be the finest mechanic for your body-machine!

Knowing Fundamentals of Nutrition: The Foundation of Yum

Consider yourself creating a LEGO castle. To make it robust and amazing, you must use several kinds of blocks, right? Your body is exactly the same, then. To be healthy and full of vitality, it requires several kinds of nutrients. Let's gather the top performers:

1. One could see these as your castle's sturdy walls of protein power. They maintain your complete feeling and assist you develop muscles. Foods include eggs, beans, almonds, and chicken.

2. These are your energy blocks, the carb crew. They empower you to run, leap, and reason. Seek them among fruits, vegetables, and whole grains.

3. Fantastic Fats: Some fats are quite beneficial; don't let the term fool you! They improve everything, just like the decorations on your castle help it to function. Find them in avocados, olive oil, and salmon.

4. Vitamin Diversity: These are like the magic sparkles shining in your castle. Every one of them has a certain role to maintain your health. To receive a rainbow of vitamins, load up on vibrant fruits and vegetables!

5. Mighty Minerals: These are the unseen assistants maintaining seamless operation of everything. They abound in nuts, seeds, and leafy greens.

Selecting whole foods: Nature's Goodie Bag

Knowing our bodies' needs today, let's discuss where we might acquire these nutrients. Where would be the best? Whole items! These are foods as near to their natural condition as could be. Consider them as nutrient-dense nature's little gift packages.

Next time you're at the grocery store, here's a great game to play:

1. Pick one food item to challenge yourself holistically.
2. Examine the ingredient list.

If you find more than five ingredients or if you struggle to pronounce an item, put it back and search for a simpler variation.

Recall that it is more nearly a whole food the less ingredients there are!

Meal Planning and Cooking: Your Food Adventure Map

Though it sounds monotonous, planning your meals is actually like drawing a treasure map for great, nutritious food! Here's how to have fun:

Try to have at least three distinct colors in every meal—the Colorful Plate Game. You are obtaining more nutrients from your plate the more vibrant it is!

Sit down with your family and map out your weekly meals from the Weekly Menu Adventure. Let everyone select a dinner; it's like designing your own restaurant menu!

Spend some time on the weekend washing and cutting vegetables, or cooking some basics like rice or chicken. The Prep Party Set some music and transform this into a dancing party.

Challenge yourself to create a fresh supper out of leftovers in the Leftover remix. Like a food DJ combining and blending to produce something fresh and interesting!

Recall; fueling your body is not about perfection. It's about choosing to feel well in your gut and in your head.

Your Challenge of Nourishing Navigating:

Try these enjoyable pursuits this week:
1. Make a list of your favorite whole foods here. If you enjoy drawing, sketch images of them.

2. Set aside family "build-your-own" dinner evenings. Arrange plenty of healthful toppings and let everyone build their own work of art.

3. Try one new veggie or fruit this week. Taste like what? How did that affect you?

Jot down your experiences in your diary. What did you learn about encouraging your body?

We will then look at ways to be appreciative of the great cuisine we have access to. But just now, go forth and feed that amazing body of yours! Recall that every meal presents an opportunity to show your body some affection. Food adventurer, you're really doing fantastic.

Chapter 7: Cultivating Gratitude for Food

Hey there, food explorer! Today, we're going on a special mission to discover the magic of being thankful for our food. It's like putting on a pair of super-cool gratitude glasses that let us see our meals in a whole new way. Ready to dive in? Let's go!

Appreciating the Journey from Farm to Table

Have you ever wondered about the amazing adventure your food goes on before it reaches your plate? It's like a grand story, full of heroes and hard work. Let's explore!

The Farmer's Tale:
Imagine a farmer waking up early, when the stars are still twinkling in the sky. They plant tiny seeds, water them, and watch over

them as they grow. It's like being a plant superhero!

The Delivery Dash:

Once the food is ready, it goes on a road trip. Trucks, trains, and sometimes even ships carry it to your local store. It's like a race to get the freshest food for you!

The Store Showcase:

At the store, people carefully arrange the food so you can find what you need. They're like food librarians, organizing everything just right.

The Kitchen Magic:

Finally, someone (maybe you or your family) turns these ingredients into a delicious meal. It's like being a food wizard, creating yummy spells in the kitchen!

Next time you sit down to eat, take a moment to think about all these food heroes. It's pretty amazing when you think about it, right?

Practicing Food Gratitude Exercises

Now that we know about food's exciting journey, let's practice being thankful. Here are some fun exercises to try:

1. **The Thankful Three:**
Before you start eating, name three things you're grateful for about your meal. Maybe it's the color, the smell, or the person who cooked it for you.

2. **The Silent Appreciation:**
Take a minute of quiet time before your meal. Use your senses to really notice your food. What do you see? Smell? It's like giving your food a silent high-five!

3. **The Gratitude ABCs:**
Go through the alphabet and name a food you're thankful for that starts with each

letter. It's tricky, but fun! (Q for Quesadilla, anyone?)

4. The Thank You Note:
Write a thank you note to your favorite food. What do you love about it? How does it make you feel? You don't have to send it - it's just for fun!

Connecting with Your Food Sources

Want to feel even more connected to your food? Try these cool ideas:

1. Grow Something Yummy:
Plant some herbs in a pot or start a small vegetable garden. Watching your own food grow is super exciting!

2. Visit a Farmer's Market:
Talk to the people who grow your food. They usually love sharing stories about their farms!

3. **Cook Together:**

Help out in the kitchen. When you're part of making the meal, you appreciate it even more.

4. **Learn Food Stories:**

Ask your family about traditional foods from your culture. Foods often have fascinating histories!

Remember, being grateful for your food isn't just about saying "thank you." It's about really noticing and appreciating all the hard work and natural wonders that go into every bite.

Your Grateful Gourmet Challenge:

This week, try these fun activities:
1. Keep a food gratitude journal. Each day, write down one thing you're thankful for about your food.

2. Have a "Grateful Meal" with your family or friends. Take turns sharing what you appreciate about the food you're eating.
3. Try to find out where one item on your plate came from. Was it grown nearby or did it travel from far away?

Write about your experiences in your journal. How did focusing on gratitude change how you felt about your food?

Next up, we'll explore how moving our bodies can make eating even more enjoyable. But for now, go forth and spread some food appreciation! Remember, every meal is a chance to say "thank you" to the world around us. You're becoming a gratitude guru, food explorer!

Chapter 8: Mindful Movement and Exercise

Hey there, body explorer! Today we're going on an exciting adventure to discover how moving your body can make eating even more awesome. It's like adding a fun dance to your mindful eating party. Are you ready to wiggle, stretch, and bounce your way to feeling great? Let's get moving!

Incorporating Joyful Movement

Moving your body doesn't have to be boring or feel like a chore. It's all about finding ways to move that make you smile. Let's explore some fun ideas:

1. Dance Party Delight:
Put on your favorite tunes and have a dance party in your room. Shake, twist, and bop to

the beat. It's like your body is singing along with the music!

2. Nature Explorer:

Take a walk outside and pretend you're on a safari. What animals can you spot? Can you move like them? Hop like a bunny or stretch tall like a giraffe.

3. Superhero Training:

Imagine you're training to be a superhero. Can you leap over puddles? Climb imaginary walls? Run faster than a speeding snail?

4. Hula Hoop Challenge:

Try hula hooping. It's like giving your tummy a fun massage while you play!

Remember, the goal is to have fun and feel good in your body. It doesn't matter if you're not perfect - even superheroes have to practice!

Listening to Your Body's Needs

Your body is super smart. It knows what it needs and when it needs it. But sometimes, we forget to listen. Here's how to tune in:

1. **The Body Scan:**
Lie down and close your eyes. Imagine a warm, glowing light moving from your toes up to your head. How does each part of your body feel?

2. **The Energy Check:**
Before you move, ask yourself: "Do I feel bouncy like a kangaroo or sleepy like a koala?" Choose a movement that matches your energy.

3. **The Stretch and Yawn:**
When you wake up, have a big stretch and yawn. Notice how your body feels. Does it want to curl up or jump out of bed?

4. **The Hunger Games:**

After moving, pay attention to how hungry you feel. Does your tummy feel different than before you moved?

Balancing Exercise and Rest

Just like in a story, our bodies need both exciting adventures (exercise) and quiet time (rest). Finding the right balance is key:

1. **The Movement Menu:**
Create a list of different ways to move. Include both energetic activities (like jumping jacks) and calm ones (like gentle stretching). Pick from your menu based on how you feel each day.

2. **The Rest Nest:**
Design a cozy spot for resting. Fill it with soft things and maybe a good book. Visit your rest nest when your body needs a break.

3. **The Activity Sandwich:**

Try sandwiching rest between two active times. For example: play outside, read a book, then go for a swim.

4. The Body Weather Report:
Each morning, check in with your body. Is it a sunny, energetic day? Or a cloudy, rest day? Let your body's weather guide your choices.

Remember, both moving and resting are important for your body. It's all about finding the right mix for you!

Your Marvelous Movement Challenge:

This week, try these fun activities:
1. Invent a new dance move. Give it a silly name and teach it to a friend or family member.
2. Have a "move and rest" day. For every active thing you do, follow it with a calm activity.

3. Try a new way of moving you've never done before. How did it make your body feel?

Write about your experiences in your journal. How did moving (or resting) change how you felt about your food and your body?

Next up, we'll explore how to make all these new habits stick. But for now, go forth and move your marvelous body! Remember, every wiggle, stretch, and rest is a way of saying "thanks" to your amazing body. You're becoming a body-listening pro, movement master!

Chapter 9: Developing Ecologically Sensual Behaves

Hello once again, habit master! Our path of conscientious eating has imparted much knowledge. It's time to learn how to maintain all these amazing new habits going forward. It's like helping to grow a garden of excellent conduct by means of assistance. About to start a career in habitual farming? Let's explore now!

Creating a mindful Diet Plan

Forming a new habit is like building with LEGO pieces. You start small and keep adding pieces until something quite amazing results. Here's how to produce your opus in mindful eating:

Start with modest step tangos and then advance. Maybe three deep breaths before every meal are involved. Little actions are simple to follow and might lead to big changes.

Squeeze your new habit between two of your present daily activities. Spend some time looking at your food, for example, when you sit down—something you do regularly—and before you grab your fork—yet another everyday habit.

Get some bright stickers and a calendar. Every day you work on your new habit and mark something. See your calendar morph into a rainbow of success.

Create a crazy rhymed song or poetry to remind you of your changed habit. "I inhale; lunch is here before I bite!" Singing it makes one enjoy remembering!

Getting beyond Challenges

Sometimes we could find our new habits challenging or forget about them. That's all wonderful! Setbacks are just inevitable features of the road. This is the way one should heal:

1. **The Oops Opportunity**: When you forget a habit, try not to become enraged. Say "Oops!" then think about this chance to start again. It's like getting one more turn in a board game.

2. **The Detective Game:** Put on your detective helmet should a habit not be working. Wonder: "What made this tough?" Maybe you should try it another time or scale the exercise down in scope.

Imagine your thoughts sitting on a big, soft cushion of compassion. Instead of "I screwed up!" try "I'm learning and that's fantastic."

If you miss a habit, set a timer for when you will try once again. It's like giving yourself a success raincheck.

Respecting Little Victories

Every progress calls for a little celebration! Celebrating helps your brain to recall that these fresh habits are amazing. Try these original techniques to help you:

1. Make an absurd dance to perform daily on your habit. The more goofier the better!

2. Designed on a poster, create a "habit highway" out of the sticker station. Every time you practice, add a sticker car traveling down the road.

3. The Gratitude Graffiti: As you develop your habit, immediately thank yourself. Post these notes where you can see them for a boost of ideas.

4. Show-and-tell your growth to a friend or family in the Success Show-and-Tell.

Observing others helps you to confirm the habit in your mind.

Remember that learning new habits is an expedition instead of a sprint. Natural is if some days are easier than others. The secret is to keep on striving and treat yourself lovingly all through.

Assignment for Habit Hero:

This week try these fun activities:
1. Decide on one everyday tiny mindful eating habit you want to practice. Make it so little it feels nearly natural!
2. Plan how you will keep an eye on your practice creatively. Maybe it's a marbles jar, a flowchart, or a thread of beads.
3. Plan a little celebration for the day you have spent a whole week developing your habit.

Write down your experiences in your journal. Stressing the need of forming

a new habit felt how? Why did it prove either easy or difficult?

We will next discuss how you may use your understanding of eating practices beyond the dining room. For now, however, start developing those amazing habits! Remember that with every practice you become more and more of a mindful eating superhero. You truly do have this habit, farmer!

Chapter 10: Beyond the Plate: Mindfulness in Daily Life

Welcome, mindfulness explorer! You've come so far on your journey. Now it's time to take all the awesome skills you've learned about mindful eating and spread them like sparkly magic dust over the rest of your life. Are you ready to become a mindfulness superhero in everything you do? Let's dive in!

Applying Mindfulness to Other Areas

Mindfulness isn't just for mealtimes. It's like a super cool pair of glasses that can help you see the whole world in a new way. Let's try it on different parts of your day:

1. The Morning Miracle:
When you wake up, take a moment to stretch and notice how your body feels. It's

like giving your sleepy muscles a gentle "good morning" hug.

2. The Shower Power:

Feel the water on your skin. Is it warm or cool? Listen to the sound it makes. It's like turning your shower into a mini spa adventure!

3. The Homework Helper:

Before starting homework, take three deep breaths. Notice how the paper or computer screen looks. It's like pressing a reset button on your brain.

4. The Bedtime Bliss:

As you lie in bed, notice how cozy you feel. Listen to the quiet sounds around you. It's like tucking your mind into a soft, peaceful blanket.

Finding Joy in Everyday Moments

Life is full of tiny, amazing moments. Mindfulness helps us notice and enjoy them. It's like being on a treasure hunt for happiness all day long!

1. The Smile Collector:
Try to spot smiles throughout your day. Count how many you see. It's like gathering little bits of sunshine!

2. The Nature Detective:
When you're outside, look for something beautiful in nature. Maybe it's a cool cloud shape or a pretty leaf. It's like Mother Nature is playing hide-and-seek with you.

3. The Gratitude Game:
Before bed, think of three good things that happened today. They can be big or small. It's like giving your day a happy high-five before you sleep.

4. The Kindness Sprinkler:

Do one small kind thing each day. Hold a door, share a snack, or give a compliment. It's like sprinkling kindness confetti wherever you go!

Creating a Balanced Lifestyle

Balance is like being a tightrope walker in the circus of life. It's about finding the right mix of all the different things that make you happy and healthy.

1. **The Activity Rainbow:**
Imagine your day as a rainbow. Each color is a different kind of activity (like school, play, rest, family time). Try to include all the colors each day for a balanced rainbow life!

2. **The Mood Weather Report:**
Check in with your feelings throughout the day. Are you feeling sunny, cloudy, or maybe a bit stormy? Knowing your emotional weather helps you take care of yourself better.

3. The Screen-Free Safari:

Set aside some time each day to explore life without screens. What new things can you discover when you're not looking at a phone or TV?

4. The Zen Zone:

Create a special quiet spot in your home. Visit it when you need a moment of calm. It's like having your own personal peace station!

Remember, being mindful isn't about being perfect. It's about noticing the world around you and inside you with kindness and curiosity.

Your Mindfulness Explorer Challenge:

This week, try these fun activities:

1. Pick one daily activity (like brushing your teeth) and try to do it mindfully every day. Notice how it feels, smells, and sounds.
2. Start a "Joy Journal." Each day, write down one tiny moment that made you smile.
3. Have a "Mindful Day" where you try to bring mindfulness to as many activities as you can. What did you notice that you usually don't?

Write about your experiences in your journal. How did spreading mindfulness to other parts of your life make you feel?

Congratulations, mindfulness superhero! You've reached the end of our journey together, but remember, this is just the beginning of your mindful adventure. Keep exploring, keep noticing, and keep being amazingly you!

Next up, we'll have a special section with daily practices to help you continue your mindful journey. But for now, go forth and sprinkle your mindfulness magic everywhere you go! Remember, every moment is a chance to be present and appreciate the wonderful world around you. You're doing great, mindfulness master!

30-Day Guide: Daily Practices and Reflections

Welcome, mindful explorer! You've made it to the most exciting part of our journey - your personal 30-day mindful eating expedition. Think of this as your treasure map to discovering the wonders of mindful eating. Each day, you'll have a special mission to complete. Are you ready to embark on this month-long quest? Let's set sail!

How to Use This Guide:

Imagine you're the captain of a ship sailing through the sea of mindful eating. Each day is like a new island to explore. Here's how to make the most of your adventure:

1. **Daily Exercise:** This is your main mission for the day. It's like the X marks the spot on your treasure map!

2. **Reflection Prompt:** After your mission, take a moment to think about what you discovered. It's like writing in your captain's log.

3. **Practical Tip:** This is a handy tool to help you on your journey. Think of it as your trusty compass!

Remember, there's no right or wrong way to do these exercises. The most important thing is to approach each day with curiosity and kindness. Let's dive into your first week of mindful eating exploration!

<u>**Week 1:**</u> Setting Sail on Your Mindful Eating Journey

Day 1: The Gratitude Gulp

Daily Exercise: Before you take your first bite at each meal, pause and think of one thing you're grateful for about your food.

Maybe it's the color, the smell, or the person who prepared it for you.

Reflection Prompt: How did taking a moment for gratitude change how you felt about your meal?

<u>Practical Tip:</u> Place a small object (like a pretty stone) next to your plate to remind you to pause for gratitude.

Day 2: The Sensory Explorer

Daily Exercise: Choose one meal today to eat using all five senses. What do you see? Smell? Hear? Feel? And finally, taste?

Reflection Prompt: Which sense surprised you the most during your meal?

<u>Practical Tip:</u> Try closing your eyes for a few bites to heighten your other senses.

Day 3: The Chew Crew Challenge

Daily Exercise: Count how many times you chew each bite during one of your meals. Aim for at least 15-20 chews per bite.

Reflection Prompt: How did chewing more slowly change your eating experience?

Practical Tip: Put your fork down between bites to help you slow down.

Day 4: The Hunger Scale Adventure

Daily Exercise: Before and after each meal, rate your hunger on a scale from 1 (starving) to 10 (stuffed). Try to start eating at about 3 or 4, and stop at about 6 or 7.

Reflection Prompt: What did you learn about your hunger and fullness cues?

Practical Tip: Imagine your stomach as a gas tank - try not to let it get too empty or too full.

Day 5: The Mindful Munchies Experiment

Daily Exercise: Choose a small snack to eat mindfully. Take at least 5 minutes to eat it, savoring each bite.

Reflection Prompt: How was this different from how you usually eat snacks?

<u>Practical Tip:</u> Set a timer to help you slow down your snacking.

Day 6: The Emotion Food Detective

Daily Exercise: Before you eat today, take a moment to notice how you're feeling. Are you actually hungry, or are you eating for another reason?

Reflection Prompt: Did you notice any connections between your emotions and your eating?

Practical Tip: Keep a small notebook handy to jot down your pre-meal emotions.

Day 7: The Mindful Meal Prep Party

Daily Exercise: Help prepare a meal today, paying attention to the colors, smells, and textures of the ingredients.

Reflection Prompt: How did being involved in meal preparation change your eating experience?

Practical Tip: Try to include at least three different colors in your meal for a nutrition boost!

Congratulations, mindful sailor! You've completed your first week of exploration. How does it feel to be more aware of your eating habits? Remember, each day is a new chance to practice mindfulness. Keep up the great work, and get ready for more exciting adventures in Week 2!

Conclusion: Your Ongoing Journey

Wow, what a ride it's been! We've traveled through the land of mindful eating, explored the jungle of emotions, and climbed the mountain of healthy habits. Now, as we reach the end of our 30-day adventure, it's time to look back at how far we've come and peek at the road ahead.

Remember when we first started? Maybe you were nervous or unsure. But look at you now - a mindful eating champion! You've learned to listen to your body, savor your food, and make friends with your plate. That's pretty amazing, don't you think?

Let's take a moment to celebrate your victories:

1. You've become a body whisperer, understanding its signals better than ever.

2. Your taste buds have gone on exciting adventures, discovering new flavors and old favorites.

3. You've found ways to handle tricky situations, like cravings and social events.

4. Most importantly, you've started to build a kinder, more peaceful relationship with food.

Give yourself a big pat on the back - you've earned it!

But here's the exciting part: this isn't the end of your journey. It's just the beginning! Mindful eating is like a lifelong treasure hunt. There's always something new to discover about yourself and your relationship with food.

So, what's next? Here are some ideas to keep your mindful eating adventure going:

1. **Keep practicing:** Like any skill, mindful eating gets easier with practice. Keep using the techniques you've learned.

2. **Be kind to yourself:** Remember, there's no such thing as perfect eating. Some days will be easier than others, and that's okay!

3. **Stay curious:** Keep exploring new foods and listening to your body. You might surprise yourself with what you learn.

4. **Share your journey:** Tell your friends and family about mindful eating. You might inspire them to start their own adventure!

5. **Keep learning:** There are lots of great books and resources out there about mindful eating. Never stop exploring!

As we close this book, I want you to know how proud I am of you. You've taken an important step towards a healthier, happier relationship with food. That's no small feat!

Remember, mindful eating isn't about following strict rules or changing overnight. It's about making small, kind choices every day that add up to big changes over time. It's about nourishing not just your body, but your mind and spirit too.

So, as you go forward from here, carry with you the lessons you've learned. Listen to your body. Savor your food. Be kind to yourself. And most of all, enjoy the journey.

You've got this, mindful eater! Here's to many more delicious, joyful, mindful meals ahead. Bon appétit!

www.ingramcontent.com/pod-product-compliance
Lightning Source LLC
Chambersburg PA
CBHW051651250726
48653CB00007B/2600